THE ULTIMATE SELF-ESTEEM WORKBOOK For TEEN BOYS

OLIVIA, J. DAVIS, PH.D.

THE ULTIMATE SELF-ESTEEM WORKBOOK FOR TEEN BOYS

A Teen Boy Wellness Guide To Conquer Anxiety, Silence Inner Critics, Overcome Negativity, Build Unbreakable Confidence, Improve Self-esteem, Rise Above Insecurities, Achieve Greatness And Owning Your Future.

RISE ABOVE DOUBTS. NAVIGATE YOUR TEENAGE JOURNEY WITH UNBREAKABLE CONFIDENCE

COPYRIGHT

All rights reserved. No part of this publication may be reproduced, distributed, or transmitted in any form or by any means, including photocopying, recording, or other electronic or mechanical methods, without the prior written permission of the publisher, except in the case of brief quotations embodied in critical reviews and certain other non-commercial uses permitted by copyright law.

Copyright © Olivia, J. Davis, 2024.

DISCLAIMER

Please be advised that the information presented in this workbook is intended for educational and entertainment purposes only. Every effort has been made to ensure the accuracy, currency, and completeness of the content, but no warranties, whether explicit or implied, are declared.

Readers should recognize that the author is not providing legal, financial, medical, or professional advice. The content is sourced from various references, and it is strongly recommended that readers consult a licensed professional before attempting any techniques outlined in this workbook.

By engaging with this workbook, readers agree that the author is not accountable for any direct or indirect losses resulting from the use of the information, including errors, omissions, or inaccuracies. It is the reader's responsibility to exercise discretion and seek professional guidance as needed.

ABOUT THE AUTHOR

Olivia J. Davis, Ph.D., is a highly experienced psychologist, therapist, and counselor with over 25 years of dedicated service in guiding individuals through life's complexities. Specializing in working with teenagers and adults of all genders, Olivia is renowned for her unwavering commitment to helping people become the best versions of themselves.

Armed with a Ph.D. in Clinical Psychology, Olivia combines a solid academic foundation with practical, hands-on therapy and counseling. Throughout her extensive career, she has successfully supported numerous individuals facing a variety of challenges, from teenagers navigating adolescence to adults dealing with life transitions.

Olivia is recognized for her exceptional ability to nurture confidence and self-esteem in her clients. Utilizing evidence-based practices and personalized strategies, she empowers individuals to recognize their strengths, embrace their uniqueness, and navigate life with newfound assurance.

Her expertise extends to addressing anxiety and depression, guiding clients through tailored interventions that foster resilience and reclaim control over their mental well-being. Beyond formal education, Olivia possesses a profound understanding of human nature, anchored in empathy and a genuine connection with the human experience.

Recognizing that self-help is a unique journey for each individual, Olivia's holistic approach considers their background, challenges, and aspirations. This personalized touch sets her apart, making her a trusted ally in the pursuit of personal development and well-being.

Whether guiding teenagers through tumultuous years or helping adults navigate life transitions, Olivia's mission remains consistent — to inspire positive change. Her clients not only overcome challenges but emerge with renewed purpose, resilience, and an unwavering belief in their potential.

Olivia Richardson's impact extends far beyond her office, making her a beacon of support and empowerment. Through her work, she leaves an indelible mark on the lives of those she has had the privilege to guide and inspire.

DEDICATION

This book is dedicated to every teen boy on a journey to self-confidence. Conquer anxiety, silence inner critics, build unbreakable confidence, rise above insecurities, own your future, and achieve greatness. You've got the power within you!

This workbook belongs to:

_____

TABLE OF CONTENTS

INTRODUCTION — 1

PART 1: UNVEILING YOUR INNER HERO

Chapter 1: Quest for Identity: Who Do You Want to Be? — 5

Chapter 2: Silencing the Doubting Dragon: Taming Negative Self-Talk. — 17

PART 2: BUILDING YOUR CONFIDENCE AND SELF-ESTEEM CASTLE

Chapter 3: Goal Getter: Conquering Your Dreams. — 27

Chapter 4: Championing Yourself: Celebrating Victories (Big and Small). — 39

PART 3: CONQUERING THE SOCIAL JUNGLE AND OVERCOMING NEGATIVITY

Chapter 5: Breaking Free from the Comparison Trap: Embracing Your Uniqueness. — 48

PART 4: GEARING UP FOR THE JOURNEY, ACHIEVING GREATNESS AND OWNING YOUR FUTURE

Chapter 6: Building Your Support Squad: Finding Your Tribe. — 58

Chapter 7: Fortifying Your Mind and Body: Taking Care of Yourself. — 68

CONCLUSION

The Hero's Journey Continues: A Message of Hope and 79
Empowerment.

A LETTER TO ALL TEEN BOYS 83
RESOURCES FOR TEEN BOYS 84

"It's not whether you win or lose, but how you play the game."
— *Nelson Mandela (former President of South Africa)*

INTRODUCTION

Teens find themselves caught in a transitional phase, neither fully children nor adults. They navigate the complexities of both physical and mental transformations, dealing with emotional extremes influenced by heightened activity in the brain's emotion-regulating region.

Undoubtedly, for many teens, this period is marked by confusion.

Teenage years can be a rollercoaster of emotions, and one of the most crucial aspects during this time is self-esteem. One minute you're feeling like the coolest dude on the planet, the next you're questioning everything about yourself. That's because you're going through a ton of changes – physical, mental, and emotional – and it's natural to feel a little lost and confused sometimes.

Self-esteem is the engine that powers your confidence and sense of worth. The fuel that propels you through the ups and downs of adolescence.

Now, being a teen boy, it's normal to have moments when you doubt yourself. Maybe you're worried about fitting in, about your appearance, or if you're good enough in various aspects of life. These thoughts can sneak up on you, but remember, you're not alone. Everyone goes through them.

One essential thing to grasp is that self-esteem isn't fixed. It can change, grow, and evolve. The more you work on it, the stronger it becomes.

Why is self-esteem so important during your teenage years?

Picture this: You're trying out for the basketball team, presenting a project in class, or asking out your crush. Suddenly, your heart starts pounding, your palms get sweaty, and a swarm of self-doubt attacks. "Am I good enough?" "What if I mess up?" "Everyone will think I'm a loser." These are the whispers of low self-esteem, holding you back from reaching your full potential.

But with strong self-esteem, you silence those doubts and step onto the court, nail that presentation, or confidently ask out your crush. You believe in yourself, embrace your strengths, and know that even if you stumble, you'll get back up stronger.

Why should you get this book?

This workbook will be your personal guide to building rock-solid self-esteem. Through interactive activities, thought-provoking prompts, and real-life scenarios, you'll learn to:

- Silence the inner critic: We all have that voice in our heads that whispers doubts and negativity. But don't worry, we'll learn how to silence that dragon and replace it with self-compassion and positive affirmations.

- Build your self- confidence castle: We'll identify your strengths, set goals, and develop strategies to overcome challenges, all while building a fortress of confidence that can withstand any storm.

- Conquer the social jungle: Let's face it, navigating the social scene as a teenager can be tricky. But we'll equip you with the tools to build healthy relationships, deal with peer pressure, and embrace your unique individuality.

- Celebrate your victories: Taking the time to acknowledge your achievements, big and small, is essential for maintaining a positive self-image. We'll learn how to celebrate your wins and use them as fuel for future success.

- Embrace your individuality: Forget fitting in and being someone you're not. We'll help you discover your unique talents, passions, and values, and rock them with confidence.

- Set goals and crush them: We'll guide you through the process of setting realistic and achievable goals, and help you develop the determination and focus to achieve them.

- Build healthy relationships: From friendships to family, we'll show you how to cultivate positive and supportive relationships that uplift you and make you feel good about yourself.

And many more!

I want you to know that you're not alone in this, bro. Millions of guys around the world are going through the same things you are.

This workbook is your wingman, your hype man, your personal cheerleader, guiding you on your journey to self-discovery and building rock-solid self-esteem.

So, let's ditch the self-doubt, embrace the awesome, and get ready to conquer the world, one confident step at a time!

Bonus

Throughout the workbook, you'll find relatable stories, fun challenges, daily journal prompts, interactive activities, affirmations and inspiring quotes to keep you motivated and engaged on your self-esteem adventure.

PART 1
Unveiling Your Inner Hero

"The hero in you doesn't need a cape or superpowers. Your hero is you, imperfectly perfect, rising above challenge and doubt."
 — *Chadwick Boseman (actor, Black Panther)*

CHAPTER 1

QUEST FOR IDENTITY: WHO DO YOU WANT TO BE?

Let's face it, adolescence is a wild ride of emotions, changes, and the occasional existential crisis (don't worry, it's normal!). But amidst the chaos, there's an incredible opportunity, the chance to define yourself, discover your passions, and build an identity that's as unique and awesome as you are.

In these pivotal years, the question of "Who Do You Want to Be?" echoes through every decision, experience, and interaction. It's a journey of self-discovery, embracing your uniqueness and defining your identity amidst a sea of influences.

In the words of Carl Jung, "The privilege of a lifetime is to become who you truly are." The teenage years mark the beginning of this profound privilege, a quest that unfolds in myriad ways.

As you embark on this quest, consider the following aspects:

1. Embracing Uniqueness: You are an individual, and your identity is a canvas waiting for your brushstrokes. Each experience, interest, and trait contributes to the masterpiece that is you. Embrace your quirks, talents, and aspirations. Remember, as Dr. Seuss wisely said, "Today you are you, that is truer than true. There is no one alive who is youer than you."

2. Values and Integrity: Your identity is closely tied to your values. What principles guide your decisions? On a fundamental level, what holds significance for you? Integrity is not just doing the right thing when someone is watching; it's about doing the right thing when no one is watching. Reflect on your core values and let them shape your identity.

3. Authentic Expression: Expressing your true self is a powerful aspect of your identity. Whether through art, words, or actions, find ways to authentically express who you are. The world benefits from your unique voice. As Oscar Wilde put it, "Be yourself; everyone else is already taken."

Real-Life Scenarios

Scenario #1: Navigating the Pressure to Conform and staying true to yourself

Imagine a high school setting where different social groups exist, each with its own set of norms and expectations. Jake, a teenager passionate about art and unconventional fashion, finds himself drawn to a group that values creativity and expression. However, he experiences pressure from another group with more traditional views on masculinity.

Despite his passion for art and unique style, Jake feels torn between conforming to the expectations of the traditional group or staying true to his creative self. The pressure to conform is palpable, with subtle remarks and stereotypes suggesting that embracing his artistic side might make him an outsider.

Jake decides to stay true to his passion for art, understanding that his identity is not defined by others' expectations. He finds strength in connecting with like-minded individuals who appreciate his creativity. Eventually, his authentic expression attracts positive attention, challenging stereotypes and inspiring others to embrace their uniqueness.

Key takeaway

Jake's story illustrates the importance of resisting societal pressures to conform. Staying true to yourself might face challenges, but the rewards of authenticity are profound. As he navigates this pressure, Jake learns that embracing his identity is not only liberating for him but also inspiring for those around him.

Scenario #2

Remember Peter Parker from Spider-Man? Dude was all about blending in, avoiding attention, and living an ordinary life. But guess what? The universe had other plans. When he gained superpowers, the pressure to conform became a major struggle. He had to choose between fitting in and embracing his true self, the amazing Spider-Man.

Think about the countless movies and TV shows where characters grapple with the pressure to conform, from the jocks in high school comedies to the aspiring singers battling stage fright. It's a relatable struggle, but here's the good news: you don't have to be Peter Parker, or any other fictional character, for that matter.

You have the power to write your own story, one where you stay true to yourself, embrace your individuality, and rock your own unique beat.

Scenario #3

Ever feel like you have to fit in, act a certain way, or wear the "cool" clothes just to be accepted? Welcome to the land of conformity, where peer pressure reigns supreme. It's natural to want to belong, but when it comes to sacrificing your true self, that's where you draw the line.

Think about the movie "The Breakfast Club." Five teenagers from different cliques – the brain, the princess, the jock, the criminal, and the basket case – are thrown together in detention. At first, they clash, clinging to their labels and stereotypes. But as they open up and share their vulnerabilities, they realize they're not so different after all. They learn to embrace their individuality and find strength in their differences.

Affirmations

1. I stand resilient in the face of conformity. My authenticity is a source of strength, inspiring positive change.
2. I express my true self. My voice is valuable, and I share it authentically with the world.
3. My values define me. I live with integrity, staying true to my beliefs even when faced with challenges.
4. I embrace my uniqueness. My identity is a tapestry of individuality, and I am proud of who I am becoming.

Reminder

Your identity is a journey, not a destination. You are enough, just the way you are. Your individuality is your superpower. Don't let anyone pressure you into conforming. Embrace your individual journey and remain authentic to who you are.

As you explore "Who Do You Want to Be?" know that the answer lies within you, waiting to unfold.

EXERCISE ON QUEST IDENTITY

1. Interactive Activity

"My Superhero Self" - Design your own superhero persona reflecting your strengths and values.

2. Journal Prompt

Write a letter to your future self outlining your goals and aspirations.

3. Challenge

Step outside your comfort zone by trying a new activity or hobby for a week.

About Me

1. List three things that make you special, like hobbies, interests, or talents.

_____

_____

_____

2. Write about a time when you felt really proud of who you are.

_____

_____

_____

_____

_____

_____

_____

What Matters to Me

1. Name three things that are really important to you.

_____

_____

_____

2. Share a story about a time you did something because it felt right to you.

_____

_____

_____

_____

_____

_____

_____

Try Something New

1. Pick a way to express yourself – drawing, writing, or anything else. Give it a shot!

_____

_____

_____

2. Describe how it felt to express yourself in your own way.

_____

_____

_____

_____

_____

_____

_____

Who I Look Up To

1. Think of someone you really like or admire. What do you like about them?

___

___

___

___

___

2. How can you be a bit more like that person in your own way?

___

___

___

___

Dealing with Pressure

1. Imagine a time when you feel pressure to be like everyone else. How would you handle it?

_____

_____

_____

_____

_____

_____

_____

2. List three things you could do to stay true to yourself in that situation.

_____

_____

_____

Positive Words

1. Write three nice things about yourself. Read them every morning for a week.

_____

_____

_____

2. How did saying these positive things make you feel?

_____

_____

_____

_____

_____

_____

_____

My Support Team

1. Who in your life makes you feel good about being yourself? Tell them thanks!

_____

_____

_____

2. How does having people who support you make you feel?

_____

_____

_____

_____

_____

_____

_____

The ultimate self-esteem workbook for teen boys | Olivia, J. Davis, Ph.D.

CHAPTER 2

SILENCING THE DOUBTING DRAGON: TAMING NEGATIVE SELF-TALK

Yo, future heroes!

Ever feel like there's a voice inside your head constantly criticizing you, putting you down, and whispering doubts in your ear? That, my friend, is the "Doubting Dragon," a sneaky beast that loves to sabotage your confidence and hold you back from achieving your goals. But fear not! This chapter equips you with the ultimate dragon-slaying tools to silence that inner critic and unleash your true potential.

The Lowdown on Negative Self-Talk

Negative self-talk is like a broken record playing on repeat in your head. It tells you things like "You're not good enough," "You'll never succeed," or "Everyone thinks you're a loser." While it might sound powerful, remember, it's just a voice, not the truth.

Here's how the Doubting Dragon operates

- Overgeneralization: It takes one mistake and blows it out of proportion, making you feel like you're a failure at everything.

- Mind Reading: It assumes you know what others are thinking, even though you're probably just projecting your own insecurities.

- Catastrophizing: It turns small problems into major disasters, making you imagine the worst-case scenario before anything even happens.

But here's the good news; you have the power to silence this dragon and reclaim your inner peace. Here's how:

- Identify the Dragon: The first step is becoming aware of your negative self-talk. Pay attention to the thoughts that pop into your head, especially when you're feeling down. Write them down and see if they fall into any of the Doubting Dragon's tactics.

- Challenge the Dragon: Don't just accept those negative thoughts as truth. Ask yourself if they're realistic, helpful, or based on evidence. Would you say those things to a friend?

- Reframe the Dragon: Turn those negative thoughts into positive affirmations. Instead of "I'm going to fail," say "I can learn from this and try again."

- Find Your Support Squad: Surround yourself with positive people who believe in you and will lift you up when you're feeling down. Talk to your friends, family, or a trusted mentor.

Real-Life Stories

Story #1 : A Tale of Triumph Over Doubt

Meet Chris, a teenager who loved painting but doubted his artistic abilities. His Doubting Dragon whispered, "Your art isn't good enough for others to appreciate." This dragon almost convinced Chris to keep his art hidden.

One day, Chris decided to face his dragon. He challenged negative thoughts by reminding himself that art is subjective, and his unique style is valuable. With self-compassion, he embraced his imperfections, recognizing that every stroke was a step towards improvement.

Chris exhibited his paintings at a local art fair. To his surprise, people admired his work! Overcoming self-doubt not only allowed him to share his passion but also brought him a sense of accomplishment.

Story #2 : From Doubting Dragon to Fearless Flyer

Taylor, my fourteen years old son used to be the Doubting Dragon's favorite target. Every time he tried something new, it would whisper, "You're not good enough," or "You'll just fail anyway." He let it hold him back from so many opportunities – joining the school play, trying out for the soccer team, even asking his crush out.

One day, he decided he'd had enough. He started recognizing the Dragon's tactics and challenging its lies. He wrote down its negativity, then replaced it with positive affirmations. He surrounded himself with supportive people who believed in him. Slowly but surely, the Dragon's voice grew quieter, and his confidence began to soar.

One of his biggest victories came when he decided to audition for the school play. The Dragon screamed, "You'll mess up in front of everyone!" But he shut it down and focused on his passion for acting. He practiced his lines, visualized his success, and gave it his all. And guess what? He got the part!

Standing on stage that night, the applause washing over him, he realized the Doubting Dragon had lost. He had faced his fears, silenced his inner critic, and achieved something amazing. That experience taught him that we all have the power to overcome self-doubt and reach for our dreams.

Affirmations

1. I am aware of the Doubting Dragon. I choose to replace its doubts with my own affirmations of strength and capability.
2. I challenge negative thoughts. I am in control of my mind and choose thoughts that empower me.
3. I am deserving of self-compassion. In moments of doubt, I offer myself kindness and understanding.
4. I am like Chris, brave in the face of doubt. My uniqueness is a strength, and I am proud to share it with the world.

Reminder

You too have the power to silence your inner critic and achieve your dreams. Don't let self-doubt hold you back. Believe in yourself, take risks, and chase your passions with all your heart.

EXERCISE ON TAMING NEGATIVE SELF-TALK

1. Interactive Activity

"Thought Bubble Busting" - Identify and challenge negative self-talk by writing them down and replacing them with positive affirmations.

2. Journal Prompt

Journal about a situation where you experienced negative self-talk and how you could have handled it differently.

3. Challenge

Practice mindfulness for a week, focusing on observing your thoughts without judgment.

Identifying the Doubting Dragon

1. List three negative thoughts or doubts that often come to mind.

_____

_____

_____

2. Challenge each thought by writing a positive affirmation to counter it.

_____

_____

_____

_____

_____

_____

Doubt-Busting Journal

1. Recall a recent situation where self-doubt held you back. Write about the thoughts that emerged.

_____
_____
_____
_____
_____

2. Share a story about a time you did something because it felt right to you.

_____
_____
_____
_____
_____

My Daily Wins Log

1. Each day, jot down one thing you did well or felt good about, no matter how small.

_____

_____

_____

_____

_____

_____

_____

_____

_____

_____

_____

Visualization Exercise

1. Close your eyes and visualize yourself confidently facing the Doubting Dragon. How do you conquer it?

_____

_____

_____

_____

_____

2. Write a description of this visualization, emphasizing the feelings of empowerment and self-assurance.

_____

_____

_____

_____

Friendly Letter

1. Think about a time when a friend faced a challenge. What supportive words would you say to them?

_____

_____

_____

_____

_____

2. Write a friendly letter to yourself using those kind and encouraging words.

_____

_____

_____

_____

_____

PART 2
Building Your Confidence and Self-Esteem Castle

"Nobody can make you feel inferior without your consent."

- Eleanor Roosevelt (former First Lady of the United States)

CHAPTER 3

GOAL GETTER: CONQUERING YOUR DREAMS

Ever gaze at the night sky, mesmerized by the twinkling stars, and think, "Man, I wish I could reach for something that big and amazing?" Well, guess what? You totally can! That's the power of having dreams – big, bold visions of what you want to achieve in life.

But dreams are just the starting point. To truly conquer those dreams, you need to transform into a Goal Getter, a relentless pursuer of your aspirations. In this chapter, we'll unleash your inner Goal Getter, the unstoppable force who transforms wild dreams into epic realities.

Dream Big, Aim High

Forget the naysayers who tell you to "be realistic." Your teenage years are the perfect time to set your sights on the moon, even if you land among the stars. Do you dream of becoming a renowned musician, a groundbreaking scientist, or the next LeBron James? Write it down, shout it from the rooftops, and believe in it with every fiber of your being.

Chart Your Course

Having a dream is awesome, but without a plan, it's just a wisp of smoke in the wind. So, grab your metaphorical compass and map out your journey. Break down your big dream into smaller, achievable steps. Research, learn new skills, connect with mentors, and most importantly, never stop asking questions.

Remember, every epic adventure starts with a single step.

Embrace the Hustle

Reaching your goals won't be a walk in the park (unless your dream is to become a park ranger, in which case, kudos!). There will be obstacles, setbacks, and moments when you just want to curl up under a blanket and forget the world.

But here's the secret weapon of every Goal Getter: **Perseverance**

Think about Michael Jordan, one of the greatest basketball players of all time. He famously missed over 9,000 shots and lost hundreds of games in his career. But did he give up? Heck no! He used those setbacks as fuel to push himself harder and become the legend he is today.

The Goal Getter Mindset

Picture a champion athlete training tirelessly for the big game, a musician mastering their instrument note by note, or an entrepreneur pouring their heart and soul into building their dream business. These individuals share a powerful mindset: they are goal-oriented, determined, and resilient.

Here's what makes a Goal Getter tick:

- Crystal Clear Vision: They know exactly what they want to achieve and can see it clearly in their mind's eye.

- Laser Focus: They channel their energy and attention towards their goals, avoiding distractions and temptations.

- Undeterred by Obstacles: They view challenges as opportunities to learn and grow, never giving up even when things get tough.

- Passionate Action: They don't just dream, they do. They take consistent action, one step at a time, towards their goals.

- Embrace of Growth: They understand that success is a journey, not a destination. They continuously learn, adapt, and improve along the way.

Overcoming Setbacks

The road to achieving your dreams won't be smooth. There will be bumps, detours, and maybe even a few potholes along the way. But remember, setbacks are not failures; they're learning experiences.

Here's how to bounce back stronger:

- Acknowledge the Challenge: Don't ignore the setback, but don't let it define you either. Face it head-on and learn from it.

- Maintain a Positive Mindset: Don't let negativity drag you down. Focus on what you can control and keep your eyes on your goal.

- Seek Support: Talk to friends, family, or a mentor for encouragement and advice.

- Adjust Your Strategy: Sometimes, you need to change your approach to overcome a hurdle. Be flexible and adapt your plan as needed.

- Celebrate Small Wins: Every step forward, no matter how small, is a victory. Acknowledge your progress and stay motivated.

Real-Life Stories

Story #1 : The Power of Perseverance

Michael Jordan, the legendary basketball player, wasn't always a slam-dunking superstar. He was actually cut from his high school basketball team! But instead of letting this setback define him, he used it as fuel for his determination. He practiced harder, honed his skills, and eventually became one of the greatest basketball players of all time.

Think about the band Coldplay. Their first album wasn't an instant hit, but they didn't give up. They kept writing, performing, and refining their sound. Their perseverance paid off, and they went on to become one of the most successful bands in the world.

Story #2: Entrepreneurial Grit

Now, let's explore the entrepreneurial world with the story of Steve Jobs. After being ousted from Apple, the company he co-founded, Jobs faced a formidable setback. However, his unwavering belief in his vision led him to later return and reshape the tech industry with iconic products like the iPhone.

Story #3: Musical Resilience

Take a musical interlude with the story of The Beatles. Before achieving global fame, they were rejected by several record labels. Undeterred, they continued refining their craft, eventually becoming one of the most influential bands in history. Their journey epitomizes the resilience needed to turn setbacks into comebacks.

Affirmations

1. I am the architect of my dreams. Every step forward is a triumph, no matter how small.
2. Setbacks are stepping stones to success. I persevere in the face of challenges, knowing they lead to growth.
3. Rejections are not the end but a detour. I learn, adapt, and keep moving towards my goals.
4. Setbacks do not define me. They refine me. I persist in the pursuit of my dreams.

Reminder

You have the capability to accomplish anything you decide to focus on. Don't let anyone dim your light or tell you your dreams are impossible. Believe in yourself, work hard, persevere through challenges, and remember, the only limits are the ones you set for yourself

EXERCISE ON TAMING CONQUERING YOUR DREAMS

1. Interactive Activity

"Vision Board Extravaganza" - Create a visual representation of your goals and aspirations.

2. Journal Prompt

Set a SMART goal for yourself and write down a detailed plan to achieve it.

3. Challenge

Participate in a local competition or event related to your interests.

Dream Exploration

1. List three dreams or aspirations you have for your future.

_____

_____

_____

2. Break down each dream into smaller, actionable goals that can help you work towards them.

_____

_____

_____

_____

_____

_____

_____

Goal Anatomy Exercise

1. Select one of your goals and break it down into smaller, achievable steps.

_____

_____

_____

2. Create a timeline for accomplishing each step and celebrate your progress along the way.

_____

_____

_____

_____

_____

_____

_____

Role Model Analysis

1. Choose a successful athlete, musician, or entrepreneur you admire.

_____

_____

_____

2. Research their journey, focusing on moments of perseverance and how they overcame setbacks.

_____

_____

_____

_____

_____

_____

_____

Goal Celebration

1. Identify a recent achievement or goal you've accomplished.

_____

_____

_____

2. Write about the emotions and sense of accomplishment you felt. How can you replicate this success in future goals?

_____

_____

_____

_____

_____

_____

_____

Perseverance Reflection

1. Recall a time when you faced a setback or challenge. How did you overcome it?

_____

_____

_____

_____

_____

2. Reflect on the lessons learned from that experience and how it shaped your resilience.

_____

_____

_____

_____

_____

The ultimate self-esteem workbook for teen boys | Olivia, J. Davis, Ph.D.

CHAPTER 4

CHAMPIONING YOURSELF: CELEBRATING VICTORIES (BIG AND SMALL)

Hey, future legends! We've been slaying dragons, conquering challenges, and building our self-esteem empires brick by brick. But in the midst of all the action, it's easy to forget something crucial: **Celebration**

Think about it. You ace that math test, nail the winning shot in the game, or finally muster up the courage to talk to your crush. These are moments of victory, big or small, that deserve a high five, a victory dance, or maybe even a fist pump (just don't break anything, please).

Why Celebrate the Small Stuff?

Think of your life as a video game. You wouldn't just celebrate beating the final boss, right? Every level conquered, every coin collected, every obstacle overcome contributes to your ultimate victory. The same goes for real life. From nailing that presentation to finally mastering that skateboarding trick, each accomplishment, no matter how seemingly small, deserves a moment of recognition.

How to Be Your Own Hype Man

Celebrating doesn't require throwing a confetti parade (although if you want to, who are we to judge?).

Here are some simple ways to champion yourself:

- Treat Yourself: Did you ace that exam? Reward yourself with that new book you've been eyeing.

- Journal Your Wins: Write down your accomplishments, big and small, to reflect on your progress and appreciate your journey.

- Share Your Victories: Tell your friends, family, or mentors about your achievements. Sharing your joy strengthens your support system and motivates others.

- Do a Victory Dance: Get silly, shake your groove thing, and let loose! Celebrating physically releases endorphins, boosting your mood and confidence

Real-Life Story

Story : From Overcoming Adversity to Embracing Self-Worth

Nick Vujicic was born without limbs, facing numerous challenges and discrimination throughout his life. But instead of letting his circumstances define him, Nick chose to champion himself. He embraced his unique qualities, developed his motivational speaking skills, and became a global advocate for inclusion and resilience. Today, Nick inspires millions around the world with his message of hope and self-acceptance.

Affirmations

1. I am a victor in my own story. Each triumph, big or small, adds to the masterpiece of my self-worth.
2. I celebrate my wins, big and small. Each victory is a testament to my strength and resilience.
3. I am my greatest supporter. With each victory, I strengthen my belief in my abilities and worth.
4. I am proud of who I am, and I am excited for what the future holds.

Reminder

You are worthy of celebration, every single day. Don't wait for a grand achievement to pat yourself on the back. Recognize and appreciate your progress, big or small. By celebrating your victories, you fuel your self-esteem, build resilience, and unlock the potential to achieve even greater things.

EXERCISE ON CELEBRATING YOUR VICTORIES

1. Interactive Activity

"Gratitude Jar" - Write down things you're grateful for each day and reflect on them regularly.

2. Journal Prompt

Create a list of your achievements, no matter how small, and celebrate them.

3. Challenge

Treat yourself to something special after achieving a goal.

Encouraging Self-Affirmations

1. Write down three self-affirmations related to your ability to celebrate victories.

_____

_____

_____

2. Repeat these affirmations daily and note any changes in your mindset.

_____

_____

_____

_____

_____

_____

_____

Sharing Celebration Moments

1. Share a recent victory with a friend or family member. Write it down

_____

_____

_____

2. Discuss how sharing the celebration enhanced the positive impact of the triumph.

_____

_____

_____

_____

_____

_____

_____

Gratitude for Progress

1. List three aspects of personal growth or progress you are grateful for.

_____

_____

_____

2. Reflect on how acknowledging these aspects contributes to your overall well-being.

_____

_____

_____

_____

_____

_____

_____

Success Ritual Design

1. Invent a personal ritual to celebrate your achievements.

_____

_____

_____

2. It could be a dance, a phrase you say to yourself, or a small treat. Describe how you will incorporate this into your routine..

_____

_____

_____

_____

_____

_____

_____

Small Wins Celebration

1. Identify three small victories you achieved recently.

_____

_____

_____

2. Devote a page to each, describing the circumstances, your feelings, and how you celebrated.

_____

_____

_____

_____

_____

_____

If you find this book valuable, kindly rate and leave a review, thank you!

PART 3
Conquering the Social Jungle and Overcoming Negativity

"Don't let the noise of others' opinions drown out your inner voice. And most important, have the courage to follow your heart and intuition."

- Steve Jobs (co-founder of Apple)

PART 3
Conquering the Social Jungle and Overcoming Negativity

"Don't let the noise of others' opinions drown out your inner voice. And most important, have the courage to follow your heart and intuition."

- Steve Jobs (co-founder of Apple)

CHAPTER 5

BREAKING FREE FROM THE COMPARISON TRAP: EMBRACING YOUR UNIQUENESS

In the age of social media and constant connectivity, comparing oneself to others has become a prevalent challenge.

Do you find yourself ever scrolling through social media and feel like everyone else's life is a perfectly curated highlight reel, while yours is just...well, your life?

Welcome to the comparison trap, a sneaky pitfall that can wreak havoc on your self-esteem. But fear not! We're here to help you break free and embrace the incredible, one-of-a-kind being that you are.

The Devious Tricks of the Comparison Trap

The comparison trap whispers lies in your ear, telling you that you're not as funny, as smart, as athletic, or as popular as someone else. It makes you focus on their strengths and your perceived flaws, fueling feelings of inadequacy and self-doubt. But remember, those carefully curated social media posts and highlight reels are just a tiny fraction of someone's reality. Comparing your whole self to someone else's best moments is like comparing a full movie to a single trailer – it's simply not fair.

The Downside of Comparison

Constantly comparing yourself to others can have some pretty negative consequences

- Lowers Self-Esteem: It makes you focus on your perceived flaws and forget about your strengths and unique qualities.

- Breeds Discontent: You become fixated on what you don't have, instead of appreciating what you do have.

- Hinders Growth: It can paralyze you with fear of failure, preventing you from taking risks and pursuing your dreams

Why Embracing Your Uniqueness Matters

The world needs your unique blend of talents, passions, and perspectives. You have something special to offer, something that only you can bring to the table. So, ditch the comparisons and start celebrating what makes you, you!

Think about a fingerprint – no two are exactly alike. That's how amazing and unique you are! Your experiences, your quirks, your strengths and weaknesses – they all come together to create the incredible tapestry of your being. Embrace it all, flaws and all, because that's what makes you truly awesome.

Breaking free from the trap

Here's your escape plan:

- Focus on Your Own Journey: Stop comparing your chapter 3 to someone else's chapter 10. Everyone's on their own path, with their own challenges and triumphs. Focus on your own goals, celebrate your own progress, and be your own biggest cheerleader.

- Recognize the Unreality: Remember, social media is just a highlight reel. People only show their best selves online, not their struggles and imperfections. Don't believe everything you see, and focus on the real world around you.

- Celebrate Your Uniqueness: What makes you, you? Your quirky sense of humor, your artistic talent, your passion for skateboarding – embrace those things! The world needs your unique perspective and contributions.

- Find Your Tribe: Surround yourself with people who appreciate you for who you are, not who you think you should be. A supportive community can boost your confidence and remind you of your worth

- Practice Gratitude: Take time each day to appreciate your blessings, your talents, and the things that make you special. Gratitude shifts your focus from what you lack to the abundance you already possess.

Real-Life Story

Story : From Comparison to Confidence

Jeremy, a talented artist, used to compare his work to the established artists he admired. Feeling discouraged and inadequate, he almost gave up on his passion. But then, he realized he was focusing on the wrong thing. Instead of comparing his beginnings to someone else's middle, he started celebrating his own progress. He embraced his unique style, found inspiration in unexpected places, and continued to hone his craft. Today, Jeremy exhibits his artwork with confidence and inspires others to embrace their own creative journeys.

Affirmations

1. I honor my unique voice. My perspective is valuable and contributes to the richness of the world around me.
2. I appreciate my journey, recognizing that each step is a unique imprint of my own path.
3. I embrace my individual growth journey. It is a reflection of my authenticity and uniqueness.
4. I am on a unique journey, and my path is defined by the authentic beats of my heart. I embrace my purpose and stand tall in my individuality.

Reminder

You are not a carbon copy of anyone else. You are a unique and incredible individual with your own talents, passions, and dreams. Stop comparing yourself to others and start embracing the awesomeness that is you. The world needs your unique light, so shine brightly and own your individuality!

EXERCISE ON BREAKING FREE FROM THE COMPARISON TRAP

1. Interactive Activity

The Social Media Detox Challenge" - Take a break from social media for a day and reflect on its impact on your self-esteem.

2. Journal Prompt

Write a list of your unique qualities and talents that make you stand out from the crowd.

3. Challenge

"The Compliment Crusade" - Give genuine compliments to three people each day for a week.

Unique Traits List

1. List three things about yourself that make you unique.

_____

_____

_____

2. How do these things contribute to who you are?

_____

_____

_____

_____

_____

_____

Positive Mirror Talk

1. Stand in front of a mirror and say three positive things about yourself.

_____

_____

_____

2. How does this exercise make you feel?

_____

_____

_____

_____

_____

_____

Your Unique Voice

1. Write one sentence about something you believe strongly.

_____

_____

_____

2. How does expressing your unique voice make you feel?

_____

_____

_____

_____

_____

_____

_____

Visualizing Your Uniqueness

1. Close your eyes and imagine a happy moment where you fully accept yourself.

_____

_____

_____

2. Describe the feelings you experience during this visualization.

_____

_____

_____

_____

_____

_____

_____

Personal Growth Quest

1. Jot down moments where you learn something new or overcome a challenge.

_____

_____

_____

_____

_____

_____

2. How does each experience shape you as an individual?

_____

_____

_____

_____

_____

Visualizing Your Uniqueness

1. Close your eyes and imagine a happy moment where you fully accept yourself.

_____

_____

_____

2. Describe the feelings you experience during this visualization.

_____

_____

_____

_____

_____

_____

_____

Personal Growth Quest

1. Jot down moments where you learn something new or overcome a challenge.

_____

_____

_____

_____

_____

2. How does each experience shape you as an individual?

_____

_____

_____

_____

_____

PART 4

Gearing Up for the Journey, Achieving Greatness And Owning Your Future

"The future belongs to those who believe in the beauty of their dreams."
- Eleanor Roosevelt (former First Lady of the United States)

CHAPTER 6

BUILDING YOUR SUPPORT SQUAD: FINDING YOUR TRIBE

Life's a wild ride, and navigating the ups and downs of your teenage years is even wilder. Do not worry, you do not have to face it alone. Having a solid support squad, also known as your tribe, is like having a built-in team of cheerleaders, confidantes, and adventure buddies who have your back no matter what.

Human connection is the cornerstone of well-being. This chapter begins by highlighting the impact of positive relationships on self-esteem and personal growth. Your support squad is not just a group; it's a vital component of your journey.

Why is a Support Squad Important?

Think of your support squad as your personal cheerleaders, your shoulder to cry on, and your partners in crime (the good kind, of course). They're the people who believe in you, lift you up when you're down, and celebrate your victories with fist pumps and high fives.

Here's why having a solid support squad is crucial:

- Boosts Your Mental Wellbeing: Feeling accepted and supported reduces stress, anxiety, and depression.

- Enhances Self-Esteem: Having people who believe in you builds confidence and self-worth.

- Provides Encouragement: Your squad motivates you to chase your dreams and overcome challenges.

- Offers Safe Space: You can be yourself, express your feelings, and seek advice without judgment.

- Creates Lasting Memories: From epic adventures to silly inside jokes, your squad makes life more fun and meaningful.

Finding Your Crew

Your tribe isn't limited to your closest friends. It can include family members, mentors, teachers, coaches, or even online communities that share your interests.

Here's how to find your people:

- Connect with shared passions: Join clubs, sports teams, or online forums related to your hobbies and interests. You'll instantly connect with people who share your vibe.

- Be open and approachable: Don't be afraid to put yourself out there and strike up conversations with people you find interesting.

- Be yourself: Authenticity attracts the right kind of people. Let your unique personality shine through, and the ones who truly appreciate you will gravitate towards you.

- Nurture your connections: Building strong relationships takes time and effort. Invest in your friendships by spending quality time with your tribe, being a good listener, and offering support when they need it.

Navigating Difficult Situations

Even the best tribes have their occasional squabbles.

Here's how to handle tough situations with your crew:

- Communicate openly and honestly: Talk about your feelings and concerns in a calm and respectful manner.

- Listen actively: Try to understand the other person's perspective, even if you don't agree with it.

- Compromise: Be willing to meet halfway and find solutions that work for everyone.

- Seek help if needed: If you're struggling to resolve a conflict on your own, don't hesitate to talk to a trusted adult or counselor.

Real-Life Stories

Story #1 : The Power of Positive Connections

Omar was a shy kid who often felt isolated. He joined the school's robotics club and found his tribe in a group of quirky, passionate individuals who shared his love for technology. They encouraged him to step outside his comfort zone, helped him overcome his self-doubt, and celebrated his unique talents. With their support, Omar blossomed, becoming a confident leader in the club and making lifelong friendships.

Story #2: The Strength of Friendship

Consider the story of Steve and Mark, lifelong friends who faced challenges together. When Steve experienced a personal setback, Mark's unwavering support played a crucial role in Steve's ability to bounce back. This story illustrates how healthy relationships can be a source of strength during tough times.

Story #3: Navigating Difficult Friendships

Leo had a close group of friends, but lately, they'd been making fun of his love for poetry. He felt excluded and judged, and his self-esteem took a hit. Leo decided to talk to his older brother, who advised him to have an honest conversation with his friends. Leo expressed his feelings and explained how their behavior made him feel. Surprisingly, his friends apologized and admitted they were just trying to be playful. They agreed to be more respectful of his interests, and Leo felt a sense of relief and renewed connection with his friends.

Affirmations

1. I navigate challenges with resilience and open communication, strengthening my connections.
2. I cultivate relationships that bring out the best in me and others.
3. I am surrounded by a support squad that uplifts me, and I contribute positively to the lives of those around me.
4. I am grateful for the amazing people in my life.

Reminder

Building a strong support squad takes time and effort. Be patient, nurture your relationships, and don't be afraid to reach out for help when you need it. Your tribe is there to support you through thick and thin, so lean on them and cherish them.

EXERCISE ON FINDING YOUR TRIBE

1. Interactive Activity

"Circle of Trust Map" - Identify and connect with people who support and believe in you.

2. Journal Prompt

Write a letter of appreciation to someone who has been a positive influence in your life.

3. Challenge

Spend quality time with friends and family who make you feel good about yourself.

Best Traits in Friends

1. Write down three things you like in a good friend.

_____

_____

_____

2. How do these traits make your connections strong and positive?

_____

_____

_____

_____

_____

_____

Affirmations

1. I navigate challenges with resilience and open communication, strengthening my connections.
2. I cultivate relationships that bring out the best in me and others.
3. I am surrounded by a support squad that uplifts me, and I contribute positively to the lives of those around me.
4. I am grateful for the amazing people in my life.

Reminder

Building a strong support squad takes time and effort. Be patient, nurture your relationships, and don't be afraid to reach out for help when you need it. Your tribe is there to support you through thick and thin, so lean on them and cherish them.

EXERCISE ON FINDING YOUR TRIBE

1. Interactive Activity

"Circle of Trust Map" - Identify and connect with people who support and believe in you.

2. Journal Prompt

Write a letter of appreciation to someone who has been a positive influence in your life.

3. Challenge

Spend quality time with friends and family who make you feel good about yourself.

Best Traits in Friends

1. Write down three things you like in a good friend.

_____

_____

_____

2. How do these traits make your connections strong and positive?

_____

_____

_____

_____

_____

_____

Thank You Note

1. Pick someone who helps and supports you.

_____

_____

_____

2. Write a thank-you note, mentioning what you appreciate about them.

_____

_____

_____

_____

_____

_____

_____

Your Personal Rules

1. List three things that are important to you in a relationship.

_____

_____

_____

2. How can telling others about these things make your connections better?

_____

_____

_____

_____

_____

_____

Happy Interaction Journal

1. Write about a time recently when you felt really happy with a friend.

_____

_____

_____

_____

_____

2. How does this friend make your life better?

_____

_____

_____

_____

_____

Your Positive Impact

1. Think about how you help your friends.

_____

_____

_____

_____

_____

_____

_____

2. Write down three things you do that make your friends feel good.

_____

_____

CHAPTER 7

FORTIFYING YOUR MIND AND BODY: TAKING CARE OF YOURSELF

Welcome to a chapter dedicated to the pillars of your well-being – your mind and body. In this exploration, we delve into the importance of self-care, understanding that nurturing both your mental and physical health is fundamental to building and sustaining strong self-esteem.

Taking care of yourself isn't a luxury, it's necessary for a healthy and happy life. This chapter starts by emphasizing the symbiotic relationship between your mental and physical well-being, and the positive impact it has on your overall self-esteem.

Why is Self-Care Important?

Think of it this way: if you constantly push your body and mind to the limit without giving them a break, they'll eventually say, "Enough is enough!" and rebel through stress, anxiety, or even physical illness.

Self-care helps you:
- Boost your energy levels: Feeling good physically translates to feeling good mentally, giving you the stamina to tackle your goals.

- Improve your mood: Taking care of yourself reduces stress and anxiety, leading to a more positive and optimistic outlook.

- Sharpen your focus: When your mind is well-rested and your body is healthy, you can concentrate better and learn more effectively.

- Build your self-esteem: Prioritizing your well-being shows yourself that you're worth taking care of, which boosts your confidence and self-worth.

Gearing Up for Self-Care

Self-care isn't a one-size-fits-all deal. What works for your best friend might not work for you. The key is to Discover activities that feed your mind, body, and soul.

Here are some suggestions to kickstart your journey:
- Physical Activities: Get your heart pumping with sports, exercise, or simply going for a walk in nature.

- Mental Wellness: Practice mindfulness through meditation, journaling, or spending time in quiet reflection.

- Healthy Eating: Fuel your body with nutritious foods and stay hydrated.

- Quality Sleep: Aim for 7-8 hours of sleep each night to recharge your mind and body.

- Do Something You Enjoy: Make time for hobbies, activities, and passions that bring you joy

- Connect with others: Spend time with loved ones, participate in clubs, or volunteer in your community.

Real-Life Stories

Story #1 : From Burnout to Balance

Alex was a high-achieving student who juggled academics, extracurricular activities, and a part-time job. He pushed himself constantly, neglecting his sleep, diet, and social life. Eventually, the stress took its toll. He felt exhausted, overwhelmed, and on the verge of burnout.

Recognizing the signs, Alex decided to prioritize self-care. He started incorporating exercise, healthy meals, and relaxation techniques into her routine. He also learned to say no to commitments that drained his energy. Slowly but surely, Alex found a healthy balance, his energy levels increased, and his overall well-being improved significantly.

Story #2: From Struggles to Strength

Liam, a talented athlete, pushed himself to the limit in training, neglecting his sleep and proper nutrition. This led to physical injuries and anxiety, forcing him to take a break from his sport. During this time, Liam focused on self-care. He adopted healthy eating habits, started practicing mindfulness, and sought therapy to manage his anxiety. Slowly, he regained his physical and mental strength, returning to his sport with a renewed appreciation for self-care and a healthier approach to training

Story #3: The Triumph of Self-Care

Consider the story of Joel, a teenager who faced mental health challenges. By prioritizing self-care, including therapy, healthy habits, and mindfulness, Joe not only overcame his struggles but discovered newfound strength and resilience. His journey illustrates the transformative power of prioritizing mental well-being.

Affirmations

1. I am committed to taking care of my mind and body.
2. I deserve to feel healthy, happy, and fulfilled.
3. I prioritize my well-being and make choices that nourish me.
4. I am strong, resilient, and capable of achieving anything I set my mind to.

Reminder

Self-care is not selfish, it's essential. By taking care of yourself, you're investing in your future happiness, health, and success. So, prioritize your well-being, listen to your body's needs, and don't be afraid to put yourself first sometimes. You deserve it!

EXERCISE ON FINDING YOUR TRIBE

1. Interactive Activity

"Healthy Habits Challenge" - Track your progress in developing healthy habits like eating well, exercising, and getting enough sleep.

2. Journal Prompt

Write down your thoughts and feelings when you're stressed and identify healthy coping mechanisms.

3. Challenge

Participate in a physical activity you enjoy for a week.

Daily Self-Care Ritual

1. List three simple things you can do daily for your mental health.

_____

_____

_____

2. List three simple things you can do daily for your physical health.

_____

_____

_____

_____

_____

_____

_____

Mindfulness Moment

1. Take a moment to close your eyes and focus on your breath.

2. Write down how this brief mindfulness exercise makes you feel.

_____

_____

_____

_____

_____

_____

_____

_____

_____

_____

Gratitude Walk

1. Take a short walk and focus on things you're grateful for.

2. Write them down when you return.

_____

_____

_____

_____

_____

_____

_____

_____

_____

_____

Positive Self-Talk Mirror Exercise

1. Stand in front of a mirror and say three positive things about your body.

2. Practice this daily for a week.

_____

_____

_____

_____

_____

_____

_____

_____

_____

Reflecting on Progress

1. Write about a recent achievement in taking care of your mind or body.

___

___

___

___

___

2. How did this accomplishment contribute to your overall well-being?

___

___

___

___

CONCLUSION

THE HERO'S JOURNEY CONTINUES: A MESSAGE OF HOPE AND EMPOWERMENT.

Congratulations, future hero!

You've reached the final chapter of this epic adventure, and boy, have you come a long way! But trust me, this isn't the end – it's just the beginning!

We've tackled self-doubt, slayed comparison dragons, built our confidence castles, and forged unbreakable bonds with our support squads.

Remember, you're not just teenagers navigating the wild terrain of adolescence. You're architects, builders, dreamers, and doers. You hold the blueprints to your future, and the tools you've gathered in this workbook are your mighty weapons.

As we reach the conclusion, it's time to reflect on the incredible insights gained and to stand tall in the knowledge that you are a young man with limitless potential.

In a world full of challenges and uncertainties, remember that you possess the inner strength to overcome, adapt, and thrive. This workbook has been your companion, providing tools and guidance to navigate the intricate landscape of self-esteem during your teenage years.

You Are Capable of Achieving Great Things

Pause for a moment and recognize your capabilities. You are not defined by limitations, you are defined by the boundless potential within you. Whether it's conquering challenges, building meaningful relationships, or pursuing your dreams, you have the capacity to achieve greatness.

Key Takeaways - Nurturing Self-Esteem

- Embrace Your Teenhood: Acknowledge and understand the diverse aspects of being a teenager, from body image to relationships. Unlock the code to your teenhood, recognizing the uniqueness of your journey.

- Master Your Mindset: Tame the doubting dragon of negative self-talk. Your mind is a powerful tool – wield it to your advantage. Journal your thoughts, challenge negativity, and create your own mindset makeover.

- Compassion Chronicles: Be kind to yourself. Building self-compassion is not a sign of weakness; it's a demonstration of strength. Craft a compassionate collage of self-kindness and understand the importance of treating yourself with gentleness.

- Fearless Explorer: Conquer anxiety and cultivate unbreakable confidence. You are capable of facing fears head-on. Engage in role-playing scenarios, set fearless goals, and take on the challenge of exploring the vast landscape of your potential.

- Taming Inner Critics: Silence the inner critics and nurture positive self-talk. Your thoughts shape your reality. Challenge the inner critics, set goals that champion your strengths, and celebrate the victories of your internal champions.

- Social Symphony: Navigate social pressures with resilience. Realize that you are not alone in facing social challenges. Share stories, participate in group activities, and harmonize with your social symphony to build connections that empower.

- Goal Gurus: Set meaningful goals and celebrate achievements. You are the architect of your own success. Create a Goal Guru Game Plan, engage in interactive exercises, and relish the satisfaction of achieving milestones.

- Future Architect: Own your future with confidence. Design a blueprint for success, set visionary goals, and understand the power of your choices in shaping the life you desire.

- Confidence Catalysts: Build unbreakable confidence through empowering activities. Recognize the triumphs of confidence, engage in challenges that boost self-assurance, and step into each day with unwavering belief in yourself.

- Insecurity Overcomer: Rise above insecurities and embrace individuality. Your uniqueness is your strength. Reflect on overcoming insecurities, engage in self-reflection tasks, and appreciate the journey of self-acceptance.

- Greatness Achiever: Foster a mindset of continuous improvement. You are a work in progress, constantly evolving. Design your greatness blueprint, engage in interactive exercises, and embrace the stories of those who achieved greatness through perseverance.

Self-Belief, Perseverance, and the Power of Positive Choices

Throughout this adventure, you've discovered the significance of self-belief, perseverance, and the profound impact of positive choices. Your journey to self-esteem is ongoing, and each step you take contributes to the masterpiece that is your life.

Closing Affirmation

I am resilient, I am capable, and I am on a journey of continuous growth. I am ready to embrace the challenges of adolescence with confidence, self-belief, and a commitment to making positive choices that align with my true self.

Closing Reminder

1. You are capable of achieving anything you set your mind to.
2. Believe in yourself, even when others doubt you.
3. Perseverance is key, so don't give up on your dreams.
4. Make positive choices that shape your future.
5. You are not alone, your support squad is with you.
6. The world awaits your unique contribution.

A MESSAGE TO ALL TEEN BOYS OUT THERE

Dear Teenage boys,

The world awaits your unique contributions, your resilience, and your unwavering belief in your potential. You are not just surviving, you are thriving.

This interactive workbook has equipped you with the tools and strategies to navigate the challenges of adolescence and build a fulfilling life. Use them wisely, believe in yourself, and remember, the world awaits your awesomeness.

Go forth, conquer your fears, chase your dreams, and leave your mark on the world! Embrace your journey, believe in yourself, and continue to thrive on the adventure of becoming the best version of YOU.

With resilience and belief,
Olivia, J. Davis, Author, "The Ultimate Self-Esteem Workbook for Teen boys "

ADDITIONAL RESOURCES FOR TEENAGE BOYS

Websites

The Trevor Project: https://www.thetrevorproject.org/ (24/7 crisis and suicide prevention lifeline for LGBTQ+ youth)

National Suicide Prevention Lifeline: https://988lifeline.org/current-events/the-lifeline-and-988/ (24/7 confidential support for people in distress)

The Jed Foundation: https://jedfoundation.org/ (Mental health resources and suicide prevention programs for teens and young adults)

Love is Respect: https://www.loveisrespect.org/ (Healthy relationships resources and teen dating violence hotline)

Boys' Health: https://youngmenshealthsite.org/ (Health information and resources for boys and young men)

The Mankind Project: https://mkpusa.org/ (Men's emotional wellness resources and support groups)

The Gottman Institute: https://www.gottman.com/ (Communication and relationship resources for couples and families)

Teen Line: https://www.teenline.org/ (Online peer support and resources for teens)

The Jed Foundation's Mental Health Resources for Black Youth: https://jedfoundation.org/

The Trevor Project's Resources for LGBTQ+ Youth of Color: https://www.thetrevorproject.org/

ADDITIONAL RESOURCES FOR TEENAGE BOYS

Articles

How to Talk to Your Teenage Son About Mental Health
https://kidshealth.org/en/teens/your-mind/ (KidsHealth)

The Importance of Male Friendships
https://www.theatlantic.com/family/archive/2021/06/intimacy-male-friendship-change-life/619290/ (The Atlantic)

5 Ways to Help Your Teen Boy Build Self-Esteem
https://kidshealth.org/en/parents/self-esteem.html (Verywell Family)

How to Help Your Teenager Deal with Stress
https://www.apa.org/topics/children/stress (Mayo Clinic)

7 Tips for Raising Emotionally Healthy Boys
https://www.amazon.com/Raising-Emotionally-Healthy-Michael-Reist/dp/1459731395 (Greater Good Magazine)

How to Support Your Son's Emotional Development
https://www.zerotothree.org/resource/tips-for-promoting-social-emotional-development/ (Zero to Three)

How to Talk to Your Son About Sex
https://www.plannedparenthood.org/learn/parents/sex-and-sexuality (Planned Parenthood)

Helping Your Teen Boy Navigate Social Media
https://www.commonsensemedia.org/articles/teens (Common Sense Media)

ADDITIONAL RESOURCES FOR TEENAGE BOYS

Hotlines

National Suicide Prevention Lifeline: 988

The Trevor Project: 1-866-488-7386

Crisis Text Line: Text HOME to 741741

National Domestic Violence Hotline: 1-800-799-SAFE (7233)

National Child Abuse Hotline: 1-800-422-4453

Additional Resources

The National Alliance on Mental Illness (NAMI): https://www.nami.org/Home

The American Psychological Association (APA): https://www.apa.org/

The Jed Foundation: https://jedfoundation.org/

The Trevor Project: https://www.thetrevorproject.org/

The Mankind Project: https://mkpusa.org/

Made in the USA
Columbia, SC
12 July 2025

60674941R00072